ETF Investing Like for Market Wizardz!

Learn the Magic Strategies to Defeat Mr. Market Without Doing Stock Picking or Trading - Design Your Financial Success!

By Warren Bell

T

he following Book is reproduced below with the goal of providing information that is as accurate and reliable as possible. Regardless, purchasing this Book can be seen as consent to the fact that both the publisher and the author of this book are in no way experts on the topics discussed within and that any recommendations or suggestions that are made herein are for entertainment purposes only. Professionals should be consulted as needed prior to undertaking any of the action endorsed herein. This declaration is deemed fair and valid by both the American Bar Association and the Committee of Publishers Association and is legally binding throughout the United States. Furthermore, the transmission, duplication, or reproduction of any of the following work including specific information will be considered an illegal act irrespective of if it is done electronically or in print. This extends to creating a secondary or tertiary copy of the work or a recorded copy and is only allowed with the express written consent from the Publisher. All additional rights reserved. The information in the following pages is broadly considered a truthful and accurate account of facts and as such, any inattention, use, or misuse of the information in question by the reader will render any resulting actions solely under their purview. There are no scenarios in which the publisher or the original author of this work can be in any fashion deemed liable for any hardship or damages that may befall them after undertaking information described herein.

Additionally, the information in the following pages is intended only for informational purposes and should thus be thought of as universal. As befitting its nature, it is presented without assurance regarding its prolonged validity or interim quality. Trademarks that are mentioned are done without written consent and can in no way be considered an endorsement from the trademark holder.

Table of Contents

Introduction..6

Chapter 1 - Before Investing..8

Chapter 2 - Inflation or Why You Have to Invest.....29

Chapter 3 - What is a Stock?.....................................49

Chapter 4 - Index Funds..57

Chapter 5 - The Dow Jones Industrial Average.........61

Chapter 6 - The Standard & Poor's 500....................68

Chapter 7 - The Nasdaq Composite...........................73

Chapter 8 - The Secret Weapon: ETFs.......................75

Chapter 9 - Advantages and

Disadvantages of ETFs...82

Chapter 10 - How to Choose an ETF..........................88

Chapter 11 - Understanding the Features of an

ETF from its Name...99

Conclusion..107

Introduction

Stocks have taken the world by storm once again after their recovery from the crash of March 2020. After a correction of more than 3 months, the most famous index, the S&P 500 surpassed its previous all time high.

A lot of people are now trying to improvise themselves as professional investors and are losing a lot of money, only helping those who actually know what they are doing accumulate an incredible amount of wealth that will lead to generational fortunes.

To join the club of the few investors that actually make it, you need the right strategies and the right mindset. Notice how we did not include a large initial capital. In fact, while having more money to trade with means having more fire power, it is not necessary to have thousands of dollars to accumulate stocks and build wealth.

In fact, when we started investing in stocks we only had a few hundreds to put into the market, but that sum yielded us thousands and thousands of dollars over the span of a few years.

In this book you are going to discover all the strategies that have allowed us to take investing skills to the next level and everything that helped us understand the stock market. If you diligently apply our advice, we are sure you are going to see amazing results in a relative short period of time, since this market is offering an amazing number of opportunities.

Please, stay away from all the shiny objects of the stock market. Just focus on a few stocks, study them deeply and then milk them like a cash cow. That is the real secret of market wizards!

To your success!

Chapter 1

Before Investing

If you are reading this book, you are interested in investing to generate wealth. However, there is one thing you need to do before even considering putting a dollar in the stock market. Since this book is dedicated to beginners, we feel it is important to spend the first chapter talking about an even more important topic: saving.

In fact, we believe that if you have an emergency fund of at least 6 months, you should focus on building that first before investing. Why? Because by having some cash set aside you will not have to disinvest in case of an emergency. You can easily calculate this number by multiplying your monthly income by 6. For instance, if you earn \$5,000 a month, we advise you to set aside an emergency fund of 30,000\$ before investing.

Let's take a look at some of the basics of saving money.

Everyone knows saving is a wise choice in the long run, but many of us still have a hard time doing it. To save money, it is not enough to spend less - and even this trick is not easy to put into practice. Smart savers also consider how to spend the money they have and how to maximize their income.

Pay yourself first

The easiest way to save money is to make sure you never get a chance to spend it. Establishing that part of your salary is deposited directly into a savings account or a pension fund allows you not to worry about how much money you should save each month; in practice, you save automatically and you can spend all the money you have left as you like. Over time, putting even a small portion of each salary into your savings can make a difference (especially when considering interest), so get started early to get the most benefit.

To establish an automatic deposit, talk to the payroll person at your job (or, if your company uses them, the payroll service). If you will provide the information of a deposit account other than the checking account where you receive the salary, you should be able to establish a direct deposit without problems.

If for some reason you cannot get an automatic deposit for each month (for example because you work as a freelancer or because you are paid in cash), you can decide how much money to manually deposit into a savings account each month and always follow your guidelines.

Avoid getting into debt

In some cases, getting into debt is essential. For example, only very rich people have enough money to pay for a house in a lump sum, but millions of people manage to buy real estate thanks to mortgages. In general, though, if you can avoid getting into debt, do it. In the long run, paying the money owed at the time of purchase is always a more advantageous solution than repaying a loan that accumulates interest over time.

If you can't help but take out a loan, try to pay the highest possible down payment. The greater the part of the purchase that you can deal with immediately, the sooner you pay off the debt and the lower the interest.

Even though everyone's financial situation is different, most banks recommend that debt amounts to around 10% of gross income and consider a solid situation to be 20%. 36% is considered to be the upper limit of the reasonable amount of debt one should have. We advise you to stay debt free as much as possible.

Have saving goals

It's much easier to save money if you have a goal to aim for. Set goals within your reach to motivate you to make the difficult financial decisions needed to save responsibly. It can take years or decades to achieve the most important results, such as buying a house or retiring. In these cases, it is important to check your progress on a regular basis. Only by taking a step back and observing the situation from afar you can understand how far you have come, and how much more you have to go.

More ambitious goals, such as retirement, can only be achieved after a long time. In the required period, the financial markets will change several times. You may want to research the future market trend before setting yourself a goal. For example, if you are at the beginning of your career, many finance experts argue that you should save around 60-85% of your annual income to maintain your lifestyle for each retirement year.

Establish a time window for your goals. Setting ambitious (but reasonable) time limits to reach your goals can be a great motivational boost. For example, imagine you want to own a house within two years from now. In this case, you will need to research the average price of houses in the area where you would like to live and start saving for the down payment on your new home (as a general rule, the down payments must represent 20% of the total cost of the home).

In our example, if the houses in the area you have chosen cost around $300,000, you will need to be able to save around $60,000 over two years. Depending on your income, this may not be a realistic goal.

Setting time limits is especially important for short-term goals. For example, if you have to repair your car, but you can't afford the cost of maintenance you should save the money you need for it as soon as possible, so as not to risk being left without a means of transport to get to the workplace. An ambitious but reasonable time limit can help you achieve this goal.

Keep a personal budget

It's easy to commit to ambitious savings goals, but if you don't have a way to keep track of your spending, it will be very difficult to succeed. To keep track of your financial progress, try to budget based on your salary at the beginning of each month. Allocating a portion of your income to all your major expenses ahead of time can help you avoid wasting money, especially if you split each paycheck right away as soon as you receive it.

Make a note of the different expenses. Staying on a budget is essential for anyone looking to save, but if you don't keep track of your expenses, it will be much more difficult to achieve your goals. Keeping track of what your monthly outgoings are can help you identify areas where you need to learn to contain yourself to stay within your budget. To do this, you need great attention to detail. While we should all take note of the most important expenses, such as rent and mortgage payments, the attention you should devote to smaller purchases depends on the severity of your financial situation.

It may be helpful to always carry a small notebook with you. Get in the habit of recording all expenses and keeping receipts. When you have the chance, write the amounts down in a larger notebook or an online spreadsheet. Note that there are many applications available for your phone today that can help you keep track of your expenses.

If you spend too much, don't be afraid to keep all your receipts. At the end of the month, divide them into categories, then count the total expenses. You may be amazed at how much money you waste on unnecessary purchases.

Check the amount of all payments several times. Always ask for a receipt when making a purchase in person and always print a copy of online purchases. Make sure you always pay the right price and don't get charged for things you don't want - you'd be surprised how often this happens.

Don't split your expenses just because it's convenient. If your meal costs a third of that of the friend you had lunch with at the restaurant, you shouldn't pay half the bill.
Consider downloading an app for your smartphone to help you calculate tips more accurately.

Start saving as soon as possible

Money stored in savings accounts accrue interest at fixed percentages. The longer your money stays in the account, the more interest you will earn. This is why it is advantageous to start saving as soon as possible. Even if you can only contribute a small amount to your savings each month when you are under 30, do it anyway: small amounts of money, if stored in high-interest accounts for long periods, can see their value doubled.

For example, let's imagine that you managed to save $10,000 before the age of thirty, and that you decided to deposit that amount in a high-interest account (4% per year). In five years, you would earn around $2,166.53. However, if you had saved that amount a year earlier, you would have earned about $500 more at the end of the same period, without any extra effort; a nice bonus if you ask us.

Don't get discouraged

When you can't save, it's easy to lose your mind. You may think you have no hope; you will believe that it is impossible to find the money you need to achieve your long-term goals. Remember, however, that no matter how small your starting capital is, you can always start saving. The sooner you start, the sooner you will achieve financial stability.

If you are worried about your financial situation, ask for help from an advisory service. These agencies, which often operate for free or for very low fees, can help you start saving.

Eliminate luxury goods from your budget

If you're having trouble saving money, this is the best place to start. Many of the expenses we take for granted are not essential at all. Eliminating the expense of luxury goods is a great first step to improving your financial situation, because it does not significantly alter the quality of your life or the ability to do your job. While it can be hard to imagine your days without a sports car and a Netflix subscription, you may be surprised at how easy it is to get on without those things when they are no longer a part of your life.

Find a cheaper home

For almost all people, housing costs represent the largest expense item in the budget. Therefore, saving in this area can allow you to dispose of a large part of your salary for other important items, such as retirement. While it is not always easy to move house, you should do a careful analysis of your expenses if you are unable to meet the budget you have imposed on yourself.

If you rent, try renegotiating with your landlord to snag a lower price. Many landlords want to avoid the risk of having to look for other tenants, so you may be able to get a better deal if you have a good relationship with your landlord.

If you need to pay a mortgage, talk to the bank about getting a refinance. You may be able to snatch a more favorable deal if your credit is stable. When you decide to refinance a loan, try not to extend the duration of the installments too much.

You may want to consider moving to areas where housing is cheaper.

Eat cheap

Many people spend more than they need to on food. While it's easy to forget budget constraints when biting into steak at your favorite restaurant, food-related expenses can go up a lot if you don't keep them in check. In general, buying in bulk is more profitable in the long run than buying small quantities of food; if you spend a lot on meals, you can decide to buy from wholesalers who supply restaurants. The most expensive option of all is to eat in restaurants, so try to eat at home as often as possible to save money.

Choose inexpensive and nutritious foods. Instead of buying ready-made and processed foods, try checking your supermarket's fresh food department. You might be surprised how cheap it is to eat healthy! For example, you can buy brown rice, a nutritious and very filling food, for less than one dollar per kilo.

Take advantage of discounts. Many supermarkets (especially large chains) distribute coupons and discounts at the checkout. Don't waste them!

If you often eat at a restaurant, stop doing it. Preparing a meal at home almost always costs a lot less than ordering it at a restaurant. Furthermore, by cooking your own dishes, you will also learn a useful skill that will allow you to entertain friends, satisfy relatives and even attract potential romantic companions.

If your situation is really bad, don't be ashamed to take advantage of the free food option. The soup kitchens offer meals to people in need. If you need help, consult your local authorities for more information.

Consume less energy

Most people accept the price of the bill without worrying about it. In reality, however, it is possible to greatly reduce energy consumption with a few simple steps. These tips are so mundane that there's no reason not to follow them if you want to save money. As an added benefit, consuming less energy reduces the amount of pollution you indirectly produce, minimizing your impact on the environment.

Turn off the lights you don't need. There is no reason to keep the light on in a room where no one is around. Try leaving a note on the door if you have trouble remembering it.

Avoid using heating and air conditioning if they are not needed. If you are hot, open the windows or use a small fan. If you're cold, wear layered clothing, use a blanket, or turn on an electric heater.

Invest in good insulation. If you can afford substantial home improvements, replacing old insulation with highly efficient modern products can save you money in the long run by preventing hot or cool air inside the house from escaping.

If you can, invest in solar panels. This solution is an excellent investment for your future and that of the planet. Even though the installation cost is quite high, photovoltaic technology becomes cheaper with each passing year.

Use less expensive means of transportation. Owning, maintaining and fueling a car can take up a large part of your income. Depending on the amount of miles you drive, the price of fuel can be as high as several hundred euros per month. In addition, the car requires fees for taxes and maintenance. Instead of driving, use cheap (or free) alternatives. This allows you not only to save money, but also to exercise more and reduce the stress of the journey to work.

Consider public transport in your area. Depending on where you live, you may have cheap transportation available. In almost all cities there are subways, buses or trams that connect the various areas and to move from city to city you can take advantage of the bus or train. Consider walking or cycling to your work. If you live close enough to your workplace, these are excellent choices for free commuting, fresh air and exercise.

If you can't help but take the car, consider sharing your travel and expenses with colleagues. By doing so, each of the passengers will contribute to the cost of fuel and maintenance of the vehicle. Plus, you'll have someone to talk to on the way.

Have fun without breaking the bank

While you can cut the luxuries out of your life to cut down on personal expenses, you don't necessarily have to stop having fun if you're trying to save. Finding cheaper entertainment allows you to strike the perfect balance between fun and responsibility. You will be surprised how much fun you can have with just a few dollars, if you are creative enough!

Stay up to date on events in your community. Today, almost all cities publish calendars of events scheduled in the area on the internet. Often these events will be inexpensive or even free. For example, in a medium-sized city it is often possible to visit free art exhibits, attend outdoor screenings, and attend donation-based community events.

Avoid expensive addictions

Some bad habits can ruin your savings efforts. In worst-case scenarios, these habits can become severe addictions, almost impossible to defeat without help, and can even cause harm to your health. Protect your wallet (and your body) from these addictions by avoiding them right away.

Today, the dangerous effects of smoking are well known. For instance, smoking causes lung cancer, heart disease, heart attacks and other serious conditions. If that's not enough, cigarettes cost a lot - up to more than $5 per pack.

Furthermore, do not drink too much. While a drink with friends may not hurt you, drinking a lot on a regular basis can cause serious problems in the long run, such as liver damage, brain damage, weight gain, delirium, and even death. If that weren't enough, sustaining an addiction to alcohol is a major burden on your finances.

Start from the essentials

There are some things you can't do without: food, water, home, and clothing must be your top priorities. Of course, if you become homeless or hungry, it would be impossible to meet the rest of your financial goals. Therefore, always make sure you have enough cash for these minimum requirements before you dedicate your money to anything else.

Just because food, water, and shelter are important doesn't mean you should spend everything you earn on those needs. For example, reducing the number of dinners at restaurants is a way to greatly reduce food spending. For the same reasons, moving to an area where rents or house prices are lower is a great way to save on your home.

Depending on the area you live in, housing expenses can make up a large chunk of your income. In general, most experts advise against moving into a home that requires more than a third of your income for expenses.

Pay your debts

If you don't keep them in check, they can completely ruin your savings efforts. If you paid off your debts at the minimum rate, you would end up spending a lot more money than if you paid back the sum that was loaned to you in less time. Save money in the long run by dedicating a good chunk of your income to paying off debts so you can pay them off as quickly as possible. As a general rule, paying high-interest mortgages first is the most effective way to use your money.

When you've covered essential expenses and created an emergency fund, you can safely devote almost all of the rest of your income to paying off your debts. If you don't have an emergency fund, you might decide to split the extra income between debt and the fund.

If you are indebted to multiple institutions and are unable to pay all the installments, you can consider consolidating your debt. You could sort all of your debts into one loan with a lower interest rate. It is important to note, however, that the payments for consolidated debts are almost always higher than the initial ones.

You can try to negotiate directly with the institution that granted you the loan to reduce the interest rate. The creditor does not benefit from bankrupting you, because they would lose their entire investment. Therefore, they could give you a lower interest rate to allow you to pay off your debt.

Spend in a smart way

After you've set aside a good percentage of your income as savings, if you still have money to spend, you can make non-essential investments to increase your productivity, earning potential, and quality of life over the long term. While these types of purchases aren't as essential as water, food, and household bills, they're smart choices that can save you money over time.

For example, buying an ergonomic chair for your office is not essential, but it is a smart choice in the long run, because it allows you to work harder and minimize back pain. Another example is replacing your old water heater. Even if the model you have works in the short term, by purchasing a new one you will not have to incur expenses for the maintenance of the previous one.

Leave luxury goods for last

Saving does not mean living an austere and joyless life. When you've paid off your debts, created an emergency fund, and spent your money on smart purchases that will benefit you in the long run, it's okay to dedicate some money to yourself. Healthy and responsible luxuries keep you from going crazy when you put your heart and soul into work, so don't be afraid to celebrate your financial stability with a few frivolous purchases.

Luxuries include anything that is not an essential commodity and offers no long-term benefit. This broad category includes travel, restaurant dinners, a new car, a satellite TV subscription, expensive gadgets, and more.

If you follow these steps, in a short period of time you will build a solid emergency fund. Once you have put aside at least 6 months worth of expenses, you can start working on your investments.

Chapter 2

Inflation or Why You Have to Invest

When it comes to investing, the first question everyone should ask themselves is "why should I even bother to invest?". After all, just saving up a part of your income seems a nice strategy for a bright future. However, this is not enough, because it does not take into consideration the greatest enemy of your finances: inflation.

With inflation in the economy, we mean the prolonged increase in the general average level of prices of goods and services over a given period of time, which generates a decrease in the purchasing power of money.

As prices rise, each monetary unit will be able to buy fewer goods and services. Consequently, inflation is also an erosion of consumers' purchasing power.

Inflation can have several causes, and there is no complete agreement on which one affects the most. Obviously, when the increase in the money supply is greater than the increase in the production of goods and services, we see inflation skyrocketing. Now, just consider that over 1 trillion dollars have been printed in 2020 and you can understand why there will be a problem in the near future.

According to John Maynard Keynes, inflation depends on demand, which, however, can grow regardless of the quantity of money injected if we are in a situation of full employment. In this case, in fact, demand grows due to the growth of wages.

The economist Luigi Einaudi also agreed on the negative view of inflation. On several occasions he has defined inflation as the most unfair of taxes because it affects the weaker classes to a greater extent. The increase in the general level of prices causes a loss of the purchasing power of money, because with the same quantity of money it is possible to buy a smaller quantity of goods and services.

The increase in the general price level expressed in percentage terms is the rate of inflation. Inflation has positive and negative effects. The current mainstream economy considers a moderate amount of positive inflation. For example, the European Central Bank has set a target of 2% inflation. Olivier Blanchard, chief economist of the International Monetary Fund believes that this limit could be raised to 4% to give the central bank more leeway in the event of a crisis. There is no shortage of schools of economic thought that consider higher inflation also appropriate, at least in some situations. Hyperinflation, on the other hand, is unanimously considered in a negative way.

Inflation entails the loss of value of the accumulated money, and unexpected inflation entails a transfer of wealth that is advantageous for those in a debt position and disadvantageous for those in a credit position. For example, a company or a single citizen who has contracted a debt with a fixed nominal interest rate benefits from an unexpected increase in inflation, if it also corresponds to a nominal increase in its income. The opposite happens for the bank that granted the loan, which gets back money with a lower value than budgeted. If, on the other hand, inflation is stable, the lender takes it into account when granting the loan, including the recovery of inflation in the nominal interest rate, in order to have a real positive interest rate.

Inflation in antiquity

There are many inflationary periods in ancient history. The first of these historically attested periods dates back to the Ancient Kingdom of Egypt and the Late Sumerian Period, around 2100 BC.

Another historically documented period of inflation coincided with the discovery of silver mines in Spain along the Rio Tinto and the Guadalquivir river by the Phoenicians, between 730 BC and 620 BC. At the time, Phenicia was subjected to the Assyrians and the massive importation of large quantities of silver into the Middle East caused the vertical collapse of the value of the metal, so much so that Assyria itself had to intervene to prevent further imports of Hispanic silver by garrisoning the ports of Ugarit, Sidon, Tire and Byblos.

Another historical episode of inflation occurred in Phrygia under King Midas whose mythical touch that transformed everything into gold echoes both the opulence of that people and the damage caused by an excess of wealth.

The annual inflation of 400 - 500% devastated the daily life of the inhabitants of Babylon and the Second Babylonian Empire between 580 B and 538 BC (date of the conquest of the city by the king of Persia, Cyrus the Great). Such high inflation reduced the earnings of farmers and merchants, so as to push the last Chaldean sovereigns to try to take possession of Arabia. The intent was to "mitigate" the price regime with the proceeds of spices in transit along the homonymous "spice route" in the hands of the Babylonians in the last stretch, between the Oasis of Tabuk and the city of Hegra. The failure to resolve the age-old problem of inflation was one of the causes of the lack of popular participation in the defense of the city against the Persians, as evidenced by some contemporary clay tablets.

Also during the Peloponnesian War between Athens and Sparta there was a period of severe inflation associated with recession due to the persistence of the war that deprived artisans and farmers from work and trade. With the definitive Spartan victory, at the end of the thirty-year conflict, the Laconic city was literally submerged by "owls" (from the coinage represented on the Athenian silver drachma of the period), which caused the subversion of the Spartan economy which, notoriously, forbade the use of money and the practice of trade.

During the period of decline of the Persian Empire, between 450 BC. and 330 BC, the continuous internal wars and the autonomist revolts forced the issue of notable quantities of local currency in order to pay the mercenary armies hired for this purpose.

In the period of conquest of the Persian Empire by Alexander the Great, the huge quantities of precious metals stolen from the subjugated and diverted countries in Greece, Macedonia and Epirus caused a decrease in the intrinsic value of the gold contained in the Persian Daricus and the silver of the Greek Drachma.

Subsequently, during the period passed into history with the name of "Hellenism", there was a generalized inflation of the "free currency" of the time, the Greek tetradrachm, following an uncontrolled issue of the same by the various kingdoms in which the empire of Alexander the Great was shattered.

A very serious inflation occurred during the late republican period in ancient Rome when the state, in order to continue to finance military campaigns, altered the metal alloy of the coins by lowering the quantity of precious metal contained in them.

An even worse situation occurred between the 2nd century AD and the definitive fall of the Western Roman Empire, in 476. During the course of the lower empire, there were such marked alterations in the securities of precious metal that many traders refused to be paid in money for the goods offered for sale and also many military personnel preferred payment in kind for services rendered. For example, at the time of the reign of Constantine I (312 - 337), the bronze axis was reduced to a size equal to 1/4 of the republican one of three hundred years earlier. Similar alterations underwent the silver denarius and the silver and gold sestertius. Constantine, in order to pay the soldiers, was forced to have the solid aureo minted: a coin containing a massive gold quantity. In this case, the monetary hinge of ancient Rome was represented by the Denarius, a coin that in 218 BC contained 4.5 grams of pure silver and was traded against ten bronze axes. Around 120 BC it was traded against sixteen bronze boards. The silver content of the denarius, around 210 AD was further reduced, coming to represent only 0.5% of the weight of the coin. This was offset by a surge in inflation that reached 1,000% over the years.

From Constantine onwards the denarius practically lost all value. Previously, thirty years earlier, the

Dalmatian emperor Diocletian introduced a basket of controlled goods. These were basic necessities that could not, by law, increase in price beyond a threshold set by the authorities policy, with the result that these goods were no longer available on the market, unless they were paid at much higher prices than those politically imposed. In the last decades of the empire, no one was willing to carry out the task of tax collector, a profession that was once very profitable, so much so that state officials had to be forced to do it. The emperors who devalued the silver coin were Nero, Caracalla, and Marcus Aurelius. Constantine abolished the silver Denarius because it was now devoid of effective value and substituted the Solid for the Aureus. But the Aureus contained 8.0 grams of fine gold, while the solid contained just over half of this quantity. The adulteration of the Solid traced that of the Denarius, so much so that the last Roman emperors of the West no longer even minted the solid, but the Tremisse, with a value of 1/3 of a solid, as it contained no more than 1.72 grams of gold .

Inflation in the Middle Ages

During the early Middle Ages the European economy was a survival economy, where autarchy and barter prevailed. With the monetary reform of Charlemagne, implemented around 770 - 780 AD, the lira was introduced both as a unit of measurement and as a unit of account. With this "virtual currency" , in an era of severe destitution and widespread poverty, about 47 plots of land could be bought for a single coin.

In the Late Middle Ages the Italian municipalities began to mint gold coins, and other European states also set out on this path. However, the counterfeiting of coins also began with a consequent resumption of inflation. For those who altered the currency - in any way and in any form - the death penalty was provided. A period of high inflation also occurred after 1352, when - at the end of the period in which the "Black Plague" raged in Europe, the population was halved compared to 1347 and - with the loss of about 30 million people - the peasants were able to obtain significant wage increases. Even the "War of the Roses", a civil war limited only to the aristocratic classes, from 1455 to 1485, left an inflationary aftermath in England after the Hundred Years War.

Inflation in modern history

The first major inflationary episode in modern history occurred at the end of the sixteenth century and led to a generalized rise in prices in Europe. There is a historiographical debate on the causes that determined it. According to some sources the reason was the Spanish exploitation of gold in the New World. In fact, following the plundering of the conquistadors at the expense of the Maya and Inca populations and the mining from deposits of the New World, the Spanish royal coffers found themselves in possession of huge quantities of gold, silver and precious goods that were poured into the European markets both to arm the army and to hire mercenaries.

The most colossal European monetary scam, which resulted in the total loss of value of the French currency, involved numerous mints that supplied the Ottoman Empire. Beginning in 1656, Ottoman women began to adorn themselves with earrings, bracelets and necklaces made with the French silvery Luigino. The coin was initially minted by the Paris mint for King Louis XIV from 1643. The undoubted beauty of the French coinage struck Muslim women, so much so that the demand for the French currency grew exponentially, as in Constantinople the wealthiest families were willing to pay a price even double the intrinsic value of the coin, given its silver content.

Faced with the possibility of large earnings, the French mints authorized to mint the coin were multiplied, but also mints located outside the French borders, by virtue of previous acquired rights, began to mint export coins. Meanwhile, in Turkey, the amount of luigini poured out meant that other jewels, starting with the rings of the various governors, were made with the luigini. The flood of luigini, however, depleted the French state coffers with silver, so much so that the king himself had to intervene to block its issue and marketing in 1667.

In the meantime, the sale of "unofficial" luigini continued, containing metal more and more debased by silver, so much so that a diplomatic crisis between

Turkey and France took place. In fact, the Turkish sultan issued a decree that prohibited the importation of luigini. The circulation of an excessive quantity of coins in Turkey caused a surge in the price of basic necessities and the sultan had to intervene again, in 1667 to deflate the speculative bubble through the requisition and subsequent merger of the imported coins.

After the American War of Independence, the printing of quantities of paper money beyond any control produced an inflationary spiral such that even today, in the United States, the expression "No Continental" indicates an object of negligible value. In 1791 the exchange rate between Dollar and Gold was fixed at 19.49 Dollars per ounce and for over a century it remained at those levels. The first serious devaluation of the American currency occurred with President Roosevelt, who fixed the new exchange rate in 1933 at 35.00 Dollars per Ounce, in the aftermath of the severe Wall Street stock market crisis of 1929. The end of the "Gold Standard" occurred on the morning of August 15, 1971, when the American President Richard Nixon unilaterally abolished the fixed exchange rate between the Dollar and the gold ounce with immediate effect. Fifty years later, on April 25, 2021, the cost of an ounce of gold was around $1,483.62.

A further famous inflationary episode occurred shortly after the First World War in Germany, during the Weimar Republic, between 1919 and 1924. The payments in compliance with the ultimatum of London, which required the liquidation of enormous compensation for the damages of war in gold marks triggered a perverse spiral that led to a devaluation of the currency and to inflation at stratospheric rates. Wages and salaries were paid every day so that their value was not reduced to zero. Between June and December 1922, the cost of living rose 16 times.

The inflationary spiral meant that people, as soon as they were paid, ran to buy any kind of goods before finding themselves with money without real value in hand, thus aggravating the scarcity of goods in circulation. Hyperinflation was defeated with the issue of a new currency, the Rentenmark, guaranteed by the lands and goods of the industrialists, then replaced by the Reichsmark with equal exchange rates. Weimar hyperinflation is often directly connected with the rise of Hitler's Third Reich, even though hyperinflation was defeated as early as 1924, so almost ten years before the advent of Nazism.

On June 15, 1939, the German government approved the Reichsbankgesetz, the reform law that limited the decision-making autonomy of the Central Bank and obliged it to carry out the monetary policy indications, which returned to the powers of the executive.

After World War II, the Reichsbank was replaced by the Bundesbank and totally freed from political power. The German mark became the European reference currency, so much so that the Austrian schilling, the Danish krone and the Dutch guilder were linked to it by a fixed exchange rate.

In the twenty years between 1927 and 1946 there was a hyperinflationary episode in Hungary as well. At that time there was a currency in circulation, the pengő, which began to depreciate rapidly to cope with the huge war expenditures starting in 1938. After the Second World War, the pengő suffered the highest rate of hyperinflation ever recorded in history. It was re-evaluated, but this did not stop the hyperinflation and prices continued to rise out of control, forcing the issuance of ever higher banknote denominations. The largest denomination put into circulation was worth 1×10^{20} (= 100,000,000,000,000,000,000) pengő. The Hungarian economy could only be stabilized with the introduction of a new currency and on August 1st 1946 the Hungarian forint was introduced.

Inflation in contemporary age

Chronically affected by hyperinflation were the Latin American countries in the forty years between 1950 and 1990. In particular, an emblematic case is the situation of Brazil, where inflation has practically always accompanied national history. In 1930 the democratically elected president, Getúlio Vargas, assumed dictatorial powers in 1937 establishing a concept of corporatist state which lasted until the deposition of Vargas himself in 1945. In 1942 the new cruzeiro was introduced in Brazil, divided into 100 centavos remained in circulation until 1967, which replaced the "real" at a rate of 1 mil réis = 1 cruzeiro. After a further four years with Vargas at the helm of the country, a military coup d'état in 1964 brought a military junta to the government. Meanwhile, inflation got out of control.

As a result of rising inflation, in 1967 the old cruzeiro was replaced by the new cruzeiro, at a rate of 1 new cruzeiro = 1000 old cruzeiro. After the fall of the dictatorial junta following massive street demonstrations in Rio de Janeiro and Sao Paulo, in 1984, the democratic government, in 1986, abolished the old currency and the new cruzeiro was replaced by the cruzado, at the rate of 1 000 new cruzeiro = 1 cruzado. Again, in 1989, the newborn cruzado was replaced by the new cruzado, at a rate of 1000 cruzado = 1 new cruzado. And again, in 1990, Brazil returned to using the name cruzeiro for its currency: the third cruzeiro replaced the second cruzado at par. And therefore, on August 1st 1993 the third cruzeiro was replaced by the "cruzeiro real" with a rate of devaluation so fast that it forced the Brazilian currency to be pegged to the US dollar. In 1994 the cruzeiro real was replaced by the second real at the rate of 1 real = 2 750 cruzeiro real.

As for Bolivia in 1985 annual inflation settled at 11,750%. The end of the civil war in Nicaragua left the country an annual inflation of 13,109%, while three years later, Peru experienced an inflation rate of 7,482%.

Mexico between 1994 and 1995 suffered a series of financial speculative attacks against its currency, the Peso, which depreciated - in one year - by 35% against the US dollar. Only the allocation of US monetary aid, resulting from the collapse of the profits of the US multinationals themselves, blocked financial speculation and revived the Mexican currency.

After 1991, with the end of communism, a situation of rapid loss of value of the currency took place in Russia and in the countries of Eastern Europe. In fact, in a market essentially closed and without competition, statalized and politically controlled such as that of the Soviet Union and the satellite countries, the opening to the free market regime caused a return to the regime of barter and the refusal of payment with national currencies. Russia only recovered from the financial abyss with the appointment of Vladimir Putin as prime minister in 1998. Also worthy of mention are the cases of Serbia between 1987 and 1994 and of Zimbabwe starting from 1984.

Causes of inflation

In the study of macroeconomics, the causes of inflation are generally identified in these three categories.

- Demand inflation. It happens when an excess of demand for goods and services relative to the supply of goods and services causes prices to rise, if and until production fails to adjust. It is the Keynesian explanation.
- Cost inflation. This refers to the increase in production costs, especially of raw materials and labor, which provokes the reaction of companies that increase the selling prices of products.

- Excess money inflation. Monetarist theory attributes inflation to the uncontrolled expansion of the money supply by central banks.

As you can see from the examples we just made, inflation happens when there is uncertainty and doubt in the future. If you have not lived under a rock the past few months, you know what is happening in the world and how the global economy has been damaged. Trillions of dollars were printed in 2020 and will be printed in the coming years. There is no doubt inflation will rise again in the near future and the only thing you can do to protect yourself against it is to invest. In fact, assets increase in value when the purchasing power of currencies decreases.

Now that you understand why you cannot just save up your way to a comfortable future life, we can dive deeper into how to invest in the stock market.

Chapter 3

What is a Stock?

A stock is a financial security representing a share of the ownership of a public limited company. Together with bonds and derivatives, it is part of the transferable securities investment category. The owner is called a shareholder and the set of shares in the company is called "share capital".

It is a form of financial investment, which exposes the invested capital to a certain amount of risk.

Companies need money to carry out their business activities and accumulate profits over time to carry out further activities, make investments and grow. There are two ways to raise funds: debt financing and non-debt financing. Through debt, bank loans are used and need to be repaid with accrued interest. As an alternative, corporate bonds can be issued.

The alternative to debt financing is equity financing. The collection of non-debt loans takes place through the sale of shares. In ancient times, the share was a certified piece of paper certifying the payment of its value and the possession of a part of the entire share capital of the company. The buyers, by buying these financial products that looked like pieces of paper, each paid a part of all the capital. For example, if you issue 10 shares worth $100 each and one shareholder buys 4 and the second shareholder buys 6, a total of $1000 is collected; the first shareholder pays $400, while the second pays $600. The former owns 40% of the share capital, while the latter, owning 60%, is the majority shareholder; on the other hand, the former is a minority shareholder.

The ultimate goal of buying shares is manifold. First of all, the purchase of these valuable pieces of paper allows companies to receive capital and encourages entrepreneurship; it allows the carrying out of activities as companies can cover their costs; if these activities are successful and bring revenues such that the cost of the activities is covered and a profit is generated, this profit serves the company to grow or carry out more and more activities or repay debts in the medium and long term. Finally, it serves the shareholders themselves to capitalize on the success of the company they have financed with equity.

To be precise, a few times a year, part of the profits generated by the company is redistributed through dividends to shareholders. According to the plutocratic principle, the profits allocated are divided according to the shareholding: the majority shareholder who paid 60% of the money as they bought 60% of the shares, are entitled to 60% of the profits. The minority shareholder who paid the remaining 40% is entitled to 40%.

In addition, the value of the share can fluctuate over time as it can rise or fall. The shareholder, including speculators and those who practice day trading, can also earn by reselling their shareholding to a new shareholder. For example, if the majority shareholder who bought 6 shares worth $100 each and spent $600 waits for the company to generate profits, they can see how the value of a single share doubles from $100 to $200. €. Thus, they can resell their stake for $1200 and earn $600, without needing to receive dividends.

The share is a non-debt financing as the money does not have to be repaid, but the gain for the shareholder derives from the distribution of dividends. The latter are obtainable if the business and investment activities are successful, which is not at all obvious as they can be a failure. A high dividend profit is a risky premium.

The difference between a share and a corporate bond can be found in the earning mechanism and in the risk. The bond is a loan of money by an investor, the bondholder. The company, by the bond maturity date, must repay the money with accrued interest. The bond's interest rate rises if the investment is risky (e.g. the company is already heavily indebted) or based on a low rating from the appropriate agencies justified by high debts or habitual breach of covenants. If the interests are very high and the risk is very high, we are talking about junk-bonds.

Shares, bonds and derivatives (futures, options, SWAPs) are all three parts of a class of financial products called securities; stocks are equity securities, while bonds are debt securities.

Since the shares can be freely resold to new shareholders, they are said to be negotiable securities. In addition, since they can be sold quickly they are easily liquidable investments.

Shares and other securities are traded in unofficial, private and less regulated markets and channels, i.e. over the counter OTC and, alternatively, in the public, official and regulated market created specifically to exchange securities. There are various exchanges around the world, and in order to trade shares of a particular company on the stock exchange, the company must first be registered on it. The listing takes place only if the company complies with certain requirements, e.g. have a share capital not below a certain threshold. A company can also unsubscribe from one exchange (delisting) or transfer from one exchange to another (translisting) or go public on two exchanges (double listing). When a company goes public and issues its first shares in the public market, these shares are launched through what is called an Initial Public Offering IPO.

Today these securities are dematerialized. They are no longer pieces of paper, but virtual data and the sale takes place through online trading platforms and no longer in person on the stock exchange or by telephone.

All the money raised with the shares issued is called "market capitalization", or simply market cap.

The set of all stock trading forms, in an abstract sense, the stock market, which is therefore part of the securities market (stock market, bond market and derivatives market).

The purchasers of shares can be common savers, large professional investors, other companies (eg banks, corporations, insurance companies, etc.), the State and the management of the company itself. The latter can therefore enjoy the fruits of their diligent and non-opportunistic work through dividends (think for example of a manager who wastes company money to buy a luxury car for himself). In general, workers can be directly involved in the shareholding with specific plans called Employee Stock Ownership Plan (ESOP), with which they are paid in shares from which dividends derive or the possibility of reselling them when they increase in value.

If the collection of equity loans takes place over the counter, we speak of private equity financing. Otherwise if it occurs on the stock exchange we speak of public equity financing.

In conclusion, there are several types of shares. Ordinary shares are the basic ones and, by buying them, the shareholder also has the power to vote in the shareholders' meeting when important decisions are made on the future of the company. The value of the vote is calibrated on the basis of the number of shares purchased or, in most cases, this standard is not explicitly followed in favor of the plutocratic principle: if the majority shareholder has paid 60% of the share capital, regardless of the number of shares bought, their vote alone is worth 60 out of 100.

Preferred shares give the right of precedence over ordinary shareholders when distributing dividends but, as a counterpoint, they take away the right to vote.

Although there is a hierarchy in the order of the distribution of dividends, all shareholders have the right to participate in the profits regardless of the order as there is the absolute prohibition of the Leonine Agreement.

If the company goes bankrupt and once the credit renegotiations and the initiatives to save it from inside or outside (employee buyout, management buyout, etc.) have failed, the shareholders are entitled to receive the money remaining from the liquidation of the company. The first to get paid are those who are entitled to compensation following a trial. Then come the banks. If anything remains, it then goes to the suppliers and bondholders. Finally, assuming that something remains, the shareholder's turn comes.

As you can see, investing in stocks is quite risky and it exposes your capital to potential losses. However, if you decide not to invest, your capital is going to depreciate over time due to inflation. Therefore, you have no choice but to invest. The only thing you can do is to try to mitigate risk, by studying the other chapters of this book and applying effective investing strategies.

Chapter 4

Index Funds

As we have seen in the previous chapter, investing in single stocks can be quite risky. However, not investing at all leads to a certain loss in purchasing power due to inflation. Therefore, the investor needs to find a way to invest without putting the capital at too much risk. Index funds try to solve the problem.

A stock index is a summary of the value of the basket of stocks it represents. The movements of the index are a good approximation of the variation over time in the valuation of the securities included in the portfolio. There are different methods of calculating the index, depending on the weighting that is attributed to the shares in the basket.

Different types of index funds

A distinction is made between these types of index funds.

- **Value weighted indexes**. Each stock is proportional to its market capitalization. Unlike other calculation methods, in this case the indexes are adjusted following corporate transactions such as splits, groupings, payment of extraordinary dividends, and so on.

- **Equally weighted indices.** These are characterized by the equality of the weighting factors for all the stocks that make up the index. The capitalization of the companies included does not matter, because all the stocks in the index have the same weight.

- **Price weighted indexes.** In this case the weight associated with each security varies according to its price. If the price of a security increases more than the others, its weight within the index also automatically increases. They are very simple to calculate as they are given by the simple sum of the prices of the securities that make up the index. However, these indexes have the disadvantage of not correctly reflecting the performance of the entire portfolio. In fact, the most "expensive" securities are represented more, regardless of the number of shares and the size of the company.

- **Sustainability indexe.** These indexe weigh each security according to alternative principles to economic and dimensional criteria and introduce CSR (Corporate Social Responsibility) evaluations or more purely socio-environmental analysis. Very often they are elaborated by the same companies that elaborate the major indexes, such as the Dow Jones Sustainability World Index or the STOXX ESG.

Most of the major world indexes are calculated using the value weighted methodology. These include the American S&P 500 and the Nyse Composite indexes.
Equity indexes can also be classified according to the industrial sector to which the securities in the portfolio refer or the geographical area to which they belong.

Almost all the indexes are calculated on the basis of the market price. This system, however, partially distorts reality, as the remuneration that companies give to their shareholders is not considered in full, but only that granted as capital gain. Dividends, in fact, are not taken into account and on the ex-dividend day the shares undergo a nominal depreciation which in theory should be equal to the dividend paid. Therefore, when an index based only on stock market prices records a decline, the greater the it is the more generous the dividend is. In this way, an event that is welcomed by investors appears to be negative. To give an example, on May 22nd, 2006 as many as 24 S&P companies cut dividends and the effect weighed 1.547% on the list, nominally amplifying the drops of that day. To remedy this deficiency, the so-called total return indexes are spreading. These also take into account the reinvestment of dividends and other cash flows deriving from the possession of these securities.

In the next few chapters we are going to dive deeper into some of the most famous index funds and talk about their history.

Chapter 5

The Dow Jones Industrial Average

The Dow Jones Industrial Average also known as the DJIA or Dow 30, is a stock index that hosts 30 major companies listed on the New York Stock Exchange. The DJIA is the second largest market index in the United States in terms of age and is characterized as an index designed to serve as an indicator of the economic health of the United States and the world economy in general terms.

Within the Dow Jones we find large companies such as General Motors, Goodyear, IBM and Amgen. If these companies in the index have a positive return, it means that the country's economy is "doing well". If, on the other hand, the economy "is bad", prices tend to fall.

Therefore, the Dow Jones acts as a sample of market trends as a whole. This becomes relevant if we consider the US economy is able to generate trends at a global level.

The composition of the Dow Jones

The index evaluation is often performed to replace companies that no longer meet the correct listing criteria. The composition of the index has changed about 60 times since the launch of the first 30 components, especially in its early years in the aftermath of the Great Depression.

For example, in 1932 eight of the components were replaced within the Dow Jones, and it was the first large-scale change. Due to the changes generated by the 2020 pandemic, three changes were made on August 24, in which companies Salesforce, Amgen and

Honeywell replaced Exxon Mobil, Pfizer and Raytheon Technologies.

How it is calculated

When the index was launched in 1896, it was made up of only 12 companies, mainly focused on the industrial sector such as railways, cotton, gas, sugar, tobacco and oil.

With the evolution of the economy, the composition of the index has changed. The Dow makes changes when a company loses relevance to current economic trends or when there is a very large economic change and the change will thus be reflected within the index. For example, if a company loses a percentage of its market capitalization due to certain financial difficulties, it is liable to be removed from the index.

The weighting that is carried out in the index is based on the share price. In other words, a stock will be more relevant in the index the more value it will have on the market.

This is known as Dow Divisor, a predetermined constant used to determine the effect of a one-point move in any of the 30 stocks that make up the index. The current divisor found in the Wall Street Journal is 0.14748071991788.

The Dow is not calculated with an arithmetic mean and does not take into account market capitalization, as other indexes do. Instead, it reflects the sum of a share price for all its components divided by the Dow Divisor.

DJIA Price = SUM (Component Share Prices) / Dow Divider

For example, if the stock of one company goes up from $100 to $110 and the stock of a second company goes down from $11 to $10, the Dow will increase overall, even if the first member is up 10% and the second member fell by 10%.

Historic milestones

Here are some important historical milestones reached by the Dow.

- **1933.** March 15th saw the highest percentage gain in one day, as the Dow gained 8.26 points to close at +62.10% for the day.

- **1987.** On October 19th, also known as Black Monday, there was the highest percentage drop in one day, as the index fell by 22.61%.

- **2001**. September 17th is the fourth largest drop in points in a day, due to the events of September 11th. The Dow fell 684.81 points that day, which represents a drop close to 7.1%.

- **2013**. On May 3rd, the Dow crossed the 15,000 mark for the first time in history.

- **2017.** On January 25th, the Dow Jones closed above 20,000 points for the first time in history.

- **2018.** January 4th 2018 the Dow Jones closed above 25,000 points for the first time in history.

- **2019**. On July 11th the Dow surpassed 27,000 for the first time in its history.

- **2020**. On February 12th, 2020, the Dow reached a new all-time high of 29,551 points.

- **March 2020.** Due to the pandemic, the Dow dropped below 20,000 points and lost more than 3,000 points in a single day.

The limits of the Dow Jones index

There is a certain group of economic analysts who are critical of the Dow Jones Index, as they argue for a lack of meaningful representation in determining the health of the US economy. They argue that 30 large-cap companies cannot be the basis for analyzing the country's economy, as they neglect companies of different sizes.

For this reason, many prefer to have as a reference the S&P 500, which includes 500 companies, which gives them greater scope for diversification.

To make matters worse, some critics also believe that just taking the share price may not reflect a company in the way the market capitalization factor does. In other words, the price of a stock could be overvalued, greatly affecting the accuracy of the Dow Jones index.

Chapter 6

The Standard & Poor's 500

The Standard & Poor's 500 is the most important North American stock index. Although historically the Dow Jones index originated first, this basket has taken on greater importance for investors over time. It is the leading equity benchmark for listed stocks on Wall Street and is the underlying for an incredibly wide range of derivative products, such as futures, options and certificates.

This index, created by Standard & Poor's has been calculated since March 4, 1957 thanks to the advanced and complex calculation capabilities possible with advances in the field of electronics. Before 1957, when there were still no computers, in fact, the S&P index contained only 90 stocks.

Membership requirements

The S&P 500 contains 500 shares of the same number of companies listed in New York (NYSE and Nasdaq), representing approximately 80% of the market capitalization, which are selected by a special committee. In reality, there are 505 securities in the basket as two types of shares are listed for 5 companies. All the securities in question relate to US companies with a market capitalization of more than $6.1 billion, a free float of at least 50%, a monthly trading volume of not less than 250,000 shares and a value annual average of the stock greater than 1.0 dollar.

Although most of these titles relate to US companies, the geographic criterion is still not a discriminating factor.

The companies to be included in the basket are selected through the floating capitalization method.

Originally the weights of the components of the index depended on the mere capitalization of the companies, but starting from 2005 the principle of floating capitalization was introduced. The transition to the new calculation system, due to the large number of stocks in the index, was carried out in two stages, the first on March 18th, 2005 and the second on September 16th of the same year. However, this change did not lead to a major upheaval. In fact, the S&P 500 companies with a free float lower than the total capitalization are a small minority.

The main titles

All stocks included in the S&P 500 are also part of the other extended S&P 1500 baskets, which includes S&P MidCap 400 and S&P SmallCap 600, and the S&P Global 1200.

The 10 stocks that currently have a greater weight in the basket and that together reach approximately 21% of the total, are Apple, Microsoft Corp, Amazon, Berkshire Hathaway, Johnson & Johnson, JP Morgan Chase, Facebook, Exxon Mobil, Alphabet C and Alphabet A. As regards the individual sectors, the most represented are that of IT with 20.7%, health care with 15.0% and financials with 13.6%.

Due to the large number of stocks included in the index, the numerous funds that use it as a benchmark rarely exactly replicate the portfolio of 500 stocks, since the sales would require significant costs in terms of brokerage fees. Portfolio managers usually use the synthetic replication technique. This means that they try to replicate the performance of the index with a smaller number of stocks selected on the basis of complex algorithms. Alternatively, many money managers use the very liquid futures that have this index as an underlying and that are listed on the Chicago Mercantile Exchange.

Trading hours

The value of the S&P 500 is automatically calculated every 15 seconds on the basis of the prices of the last contracts concluded in the trading hours, i.e. from 09:30 to 16:00 from Reuters America, a Thomson Reuters Corporation company.

The index code on the American markets is GSPC or SPX. It is sometimes also referred to as ^GSPC or ^SPX.

Chapter 7

The Nasdaq Composite

The NASDAQ Composite is a capitalization weighted index. The calculation of the index involves the calculation of the weighted sum of the products of the closing prices of the securities. This sum is divided by a divisor which reduces the order of magnitude of the result. For a stock to be included in the Nasdaq Composite, it must be listed exclusively on the Nasdaq stock market, unless the stock was listed at least twice on a non-US market prior to 2004 and has been listed continuously.

The index was introduced in 1971, with an initial value of 100 points. On July 17th 1995 it closed for the first time with a value greater than 1000 points. During the period of the dot-com bubble, the value of the index increased by 400%. On March 10th 2000 it reached the value of 5132.52. In the following period, the value underwent a significant decline, reaching 1,108.49 in October 2002. Until 2007, the index saw a decrease in its value. On September 15th, 2008, the bankruptcy of Lehman Brothers led the index to register a negative performance -3.6%, the worst percentage drop in a single session.

In the years following the Great Recession, the index returned to high values. On March 2nd 2015, for the first time since March 9th 2000, it closed with a value above 5000 points. In April 2015, closing at 5056, it exceeded the value reached during the dot-com bubble. On January 2nd, 2018 it exceeded the value of 7000 points and in 2019 the index had an increase of 35.2%, closing the year at 8972.60 points. On March 23rd 2020, the index touched a low of 6860 points. In the following months, however, there was a strong recovery in the index and on June 9th 2020, the index exceeded 10,000 for the first time in its history.

As you have learned in these chapters, index funds are a great way to invest in the stock market while mitigating risk. But how can you get started investing in them? Well, that is when ETFs come into play.

Chapter 8

The Secret Weapon: ETFs

Exchange-traded funds (known by the abbreviation ETF) are a type of investment funds listed on the stock exchange, with limited liability for the shareholders who participate in them with the purchase and sale of shares. Furthermore, they have the fundamental peculiarity of being passively managed since they are linked to a pre-existing stock index.

They are part of the family of exchange-traded products (ETPs), which include ETFs (exchange-traded funds), ETCs (exchange-traded commodities) and ETNs (exchange-traded notes), all three listed on the stock exchange and funded through shares.

Exchange-traded funds are a type of investment fund. This means they are an accumulation of money raised through the shareholding of shareholders. The fund is managed by a manager, to whom the shareholders delegate all management power. The ETF manager invests the money raised in the trading of shares. In any case, the profit generated by the fund's investment activities is then redistributed to the shareholder to the extent that they have invested in the fund, following the plutocratic principle. For instance, if a shareholder has paid 12% of the share capital, at each distribution of dividends they are entitled to 12% of all profits generated. If the fund at a strategic level is already set up to reinvest profits, it is called an "accumulation ETF", otherwise it is called a "distribution ETF".

The funds operate on the stock exchange as they are listed there, which is why these funds identify well with "exchange-traded": the purchase and sale of the shareholding takes place on the stock exchange, which is a public and regulated market.

However, ETFs have a particular functioning, since management is not absolutely free but has its own underlying logic: ETFs replicate the index to which they refer and therefore faithfully replicate the performance of a specific stock index or the price of a specific type of asset. Since the investment strategy is passive, the fund is said to be passively managed and the same fund can be said to be "passive".

Their management is passive but, in some cases, it is speculative. This happens for example if they use leverage, or if they exploit a bearish trend by shorting the market. Speculative ETFs that use leverage are also known as "Leveraged ETFs" and are flanked by two other types of speculative ETFs. These are Inverse ETFs and Reverse Leveraged ETFs. Typically, the speculative ones seek the maximum profit in the shortest possible time, which is why they tend to be used in day trading, which from the outset, in addition to being purely speculative, is particularly risky.

An example of an ETF is the SPDR S&P 500 Trust ETF, which binds to the S&P 500 index. Therefore, the ETF manager in this case uses the members' money to invest in various ways in the 500 companies that belong to this stock index. From the name, it follows that, at the level of legal form according to corporate law, the companies that manage the funds can be structured as trusts. However, some funds can also link to indexes that have an international breadth. More than one ETF can be linked to the same stock or commodity or similar index. For example, many ETFs follow the S&P 500 index. In 2015, there were over 4,000 ETFs worldwide and their assets combined totaled $2.88 trillion; the largest is the SPDR S&P 500 Trust ETF, which is a multi-billionaire ETF. Another huge one is the iShares Core S&P 500 ETF managed by BlackRock, which itself manages many other ETFs and is structured like a public company. Each ETF is always listed on a stock exchange. For example, the iShares Core S&P 500 ETF is listed on the New York Stock Exchange.

Each ETF is then specialized as they track a particular stock market index, a specific sector, specific commodities, specific securities, market caps, regions and may combine various financial products. If you use a region-specific specialization and indicate it in the fund name, the word "ex-" indicates an exclusion:

for example, "Pacific ex-Japan" means all of the Pacific except Japan. The name can also indicate the financial product or commodity or sector on which one focuses. For instance Oil, Gas, Bond, Energy, and Health ETFs.

The price of the shares to participate in the ETF can fluctuate throughout the day and be volatile due to the continuous exchange of shares on the exchange from one buyer to another.

In general, ETFs have lower expenses and the commissions to be paid for brokers are lower. Therefore ETFs are cheaper than index funds, even if they replicate their performance. Furthermore, as there are many types of ETF, they allow a great diversification of the investment portfolio. The basic expense for participating in an ETF is the payment of an annual fee.

Other features of ETFs

ETFs are financial instruments that choose to invest in a diversified basket by faithfully "replicating" the composition of a stock market index: when one of the components of the benchmark is replaced, the corresponding financial asset within the fund is also replaced. It is important to note that the benchmark is followed regardless of the greater or lesser convenience. The ETF will be aligned to the components and weights of the benchmark without the need for investor intervention.

ETFs are traded on the stock exchange in continuous trading, like shares and consequently their value varies continuously within the same trading day. Continuously bringing the fund's share back to the level of that of the index is the job of the management company itself, which will buy or sell its shares of the ETF due to the deviation from the index, which it should generally not exceed 2%.

ETFs are very liquid instruments, easily tradable. For amounts up to $1,000,000, trading takes place easily on the stock market; for higher amounts it is necessary to operate OTC, i.e. outside the public and regulated market directly with a market maker.

Despite the passive management style, there have been times when ETFs have performed better on average than active funds.

The total annual fees range from a minimum of 0.09% to a maximum of 1.5% and are paid in proportion to the holding period of the ETF.

If you understand the power of diversification and the value of index investing, we are sure you cannot wait to get started with ETF investing. The next chapters are going to tell you the right strategies to maximize your gains.

Chapter 9

Advantages and Disadvantages of ETFs

Being comparable to mutual funds, the assets of the ETFs are autonomous and completely separate from that of the issuer. And this makes them safer than other forms of investment: in fact, the bankruptcy of an issuer does not involve any financial risk for the ETF's assets and, consequently, for the investor.

Now let's see in detail the advantages and disadvantages of ETFs.

Diversification

An ETF can give visibility to a group of stocks and market segments. Compared to a stock, the ETF is able to monitor a wider range of stocks, but also "mimic" the returns of a country or group of countries. For example, it is possible for the investor to focus on Brazil, Russia, India and China in the BRIC ETF. Mutual funds can also be diversified, but the ETF has lower expenses and "works" like an equity investment.

Lower fees than managed funds

ETFs have much lower expense ratios than other managed funds. The costs of a mutual fund are usually higher due to management fees, shareholder expenses for accounting, service fees, board of directors fees. administration and freight charges for sales and distribution. Even if the ETF could give the holder some diversification benefits, it is always traded as a share.

<u>Dividends are reinvested immediately</u>

Company dividends in an open-ended ETF are reinvested right away. This is a great advantage for those who want to build wealth without taking out dividends.

<u>Tax efficiency</u>

ETFs can be more tax efficient than mutual funds because most of the capital gains tax is paid on the sale and in full to the investor. Even if the ETF sells or buys shares while trying to mimic a basket of shares, it will always be monitored. This is so that the capital gains realized on the transfers do not give rise to a tax burden and can be expected to be much lower than normal mutual funds. Mutual funds, on the other hand, are required to distribute capital gains to shareholders if the manager sells securities to make a profit. This amount is calculated on the basis of the shareholder's percentage and is taxable as a capital gain. If other mutual fund holders sell them before the registration date, the remaining holders will split the capital gain and pay their taxes, even if the fund has dropped in value.

Low discount or premium on the price

There is a lower chance of having ETF prices that are higher or lower than the real value. These funds are traded throughout the day at a price close to that of the underlying securities, so if the price is significantly higher or lower than the net asset value, arbitrage will bring the price back "in line".

They can be limited to large companies

In some countries, investors may have limited access to these funds due to a small group of stocks in the large-cap market index. And this could limit the purchase of ETFs by small and medium-sized investors.

The daily price may be excessive

Longer-term investors may have a 10 or 15-year time horizon, so they cannot benefit from daily price changes. Some investors may trade more stocks due to these delayed price swings. And this "swing" could lead to a situation where prices at the end of the day could be irrational.

The supply-demand spread could be high

The more ETFs are created, the more you could "run into" an investment with a low volume index. A better price could be found in investing in real shares or perhaps even in a managed fund.

The costs, in fact, could be high. Most people make the mistake of comparing trading ETFs with trading other securities, such as mutual funds. However, when comparing ETFs that invest in a specific stock, the costs are higher. The actual commission paid to the broker may be the same, but there are no handling fees for the shares.

Dividend yields

Even though ETFs pay dividends to holders, the yields can never be as high as those of high yielding stocks or a group of stocks. The risks associated with managing ETFs are generally lower, but if an investor can take the risk, then the dividend yields can be much higher.

ETFs are a great way to invest in the stock market and the advantages outweigh the disadvantages. If you want to diversify your portfolio, but index funds are too expensive for you, then ETFs are the perfect solution for your needs.

Chapter 10

How to Choose an ETF

First of all, you have to choose the asset class. Do you want to invest in stocks, bonds, commodities or real estate mutual funds? If you are unsure what percentage of your portfolio should be allocated to each class, keep reading because we will give you an example portfolio in the next chapters.

The next step is to define your diversification strategy. Do you want to spread your wealth across all asset classes or do you want to focus on a single market segment? In equities, for example, you can invest worldwide with a single ETF or focus on certain regions, such as emerging markets or a single country.

After you have decided these points, here are the characteristics you need to keep an eye on when choosing an ETF.

Fund size over $100 million

A fund size of over $100 million should be preferred. The ETF is obliged to be profitable enough to be liquidated when it exceeds a certain threshold.

Fund age (over one year)

You can compare ETFs once they have accrued a reasonable set of historical data. You will need a performance history of at least one year, even better if you can focus on an observation period of three or five years.

Current expenses

The Total Expense Ratio (TER) offers us an approximate measure of the annual expenses that will have to be incurred in order to hold the ETF. It covers the various administrative, legal, operational and marketing expenses incurred by the ETF manager and deducted from the returns. The current expense index is another terminology used to indicate a similar concept.

The difference is that the TER considers all the costs that you will have to incur to own the ETF. The OCF, for example, does not include fees or taxes on operations.

These hidden costs have an impact on the ETF's annual return, so performance data can be used to make more accurate comparisons on the actual costs of ETFs.

Tracking differentials

The perfect ETF offers exactly the same return as the index that follows. Unfortunately, however, ETFs are subject to hurdles that have no impact on indexes. ETFs have to bear the costs of operations, taxes, wages and salaries, regulatory fees, and a long list of other costs. On the other hand, indexes are a kind of virtual world ranking therefore they can calculate returns in a market not affected by the deterrents of ETFs.

The difference between the real world returns of ETFs and the virtual returns of the index is called the tracking differential. A good ETF manages to minimize tracking spreads by offering a market return that is theoretically quite similar to that of the index minus its management costs.

The impact of tracking differentials can be assessed by comparing the ETFs that follow the same index over the same period of time. Just compare the overall returns with each other over a rather long period of time and you will see which ETF did a better job replicating the index.

Liquid assets

When we talk about liquidity we refer to the actual ease in being able to trade the ETF on a stock exchange. The more liquid the ETF is, the more likely it will be possible to sell or buy it with only a minimal cost. Broad market ETFs are usually very liquid as the underlying financial instruments they hold are regularly traded in very large volumes. For example, most equities traded on the NYSE stock market are highly liquid. Therefore, ETFs that hold these stocks can be traded very quickly by paying a minimal margin fee on the price.

This margin is called the bid/ask spread and represents the difference between the buy price and the sell price of a stock. This is the same concept that applies when buying foreign currencies while on vacation abroad. You will always get a slightly higher price than what they were bought at. The differential is the price that is paid to the intermediary who offers the purchase and sale prices. These intermediaries are known as market-makers and are responsible for maintaining market liquidity.

The bid/ask differential increases when liquidity decreases and given that it represents a trading cost, which will have to be incurred in addition to the broker costs, it is always worth choosing the most liquid ETF within each category. The fundamental factors of liquidity are:

- The underlying stocks of the ETF - the more highly tradable the better.
- Bottom size - the bigger the better.
- Daily trading volume - the higher the better.
- Market-maker - the more, the better.
- Market conditions - liquidity decreases when markets are highly volatile.

Replication method

How is the index replicated by the ETF? There are three different replication methods.

The total physical replication method is when the ETF holds the same securities as the index, in the same proportion, to offer an accurate performance.

Another type of physical replication is given by sampling. However, in this case the ETF holds a representative sample of the index stocks rather than exactly the same stocks in the same quantities. This method balances the faithful replication of the index with the incurring of high costs that will have to be borne by following an index made up of illiquid and small securities.

The synthetic replication method allows to replicate an index using a total return swap. The swap is a financial instrument that pays the ETF the exact return of the index it hedges. Swaps are usually provided by institutions such as global investment banks, in exchange for money offered by the ETF manager. The synthetic replication method frees the ETF from the obligation of having to physically hold all the index securities. This is very useful especially if the securities of the following index are inaccessible, illiquid or so numerous that it is impossible to hold them.

The synthetic replication method exposes us to counterparty risk, which is the potential inability of the swap provider to meet its commitments.

However, even physical replication can expose us to counterparty risk if the ETF provider takes part in securities lending transactions, or the practice of borrowing securities from other financial operators for the purpose of carrying out a short sale. The stock lending policy of an ETF provider must be posted on that provider's website.

The total replication method is obviously an easier method but it is not always possible for each market.

Use of profits

Distributing ETFs credit income directly to the brokerage account so that it can be spent or reinvested to meet your needs.

Accumulating ETFs do not credit the proceeds but automatically reinvest them in the product itself. In other words, they buy additional shares of the ETF, saving on transaction costs, and increase the value of the investment over time.

Fund location

It is worth knowing where the ETF's registered office is in order to avoid tax complications in the future. Most ETFs are domiciled in Ireland or Luxembourg as these countries offer tax and legal advantages.

ETFs authorized for distribution in Europe are distinguished by the fact that their name contains the acronym UCITS. UCITS is a set of EU regulations that sets standards on counterparty risk, diversification, information disclosure and other forms of consumer protection.

US and Canadian ETFs are not regulated by the UCITS principles and may be subject to additional tax, legal and currency disadvantages. These ETFs are usually distinguished by the fact that there is no UCITS wording in the denomination and their securities identification number (ISIN) starts with US or CA.

Tax situation

Always make sure that your ETF has the fund status subject to the information obligation. This allows you to avoid unpleasant tax shocks in the future. The good news is given by the fact that UCITS ETFs are funds subject to the obligation to inform, but it is always worth doing a quick check in the relevant information sheet.

Currencies

Currency risk is given by the possibility that your foreign investments may be affected by a movement of the dollar. For example, if the dollar strengthens against the euro, stocks quoted in dollars, for European investors who evaluate the performance in euros, will appreciate. Similarly, a weakening of the dollar against the euro means that European investors will enjoy a strengthening of the returns on these same investments. Currency risk tends to smooth out over time and is a major concern for most long-term investors. An exposure to foreign currencies can also offer the opportunity to enjoy the benefits of diversification.

It is known that it is the currency of the ETF's underlyings that determines the currency risk. The S&P 500 ETF exposes you to fluctuations of the dollar value.

If you study and apply these principles, it will be much easier for you to choose the right ETFs for your portfolio.

Chapter 11

Understanding the Features of an ETF from its Name

One of the longest ETF names in the world is UBS ETF (LU) Barclays MSCI US Liquid Corporates Sustainable UCITS ETF (hedged to EUR) A-acc. It is almost an infinite set of terms and abbreviations.

While cryptic names may seem daunting, they usually rely on simple logic that can help you figure out if the ETF is right for you. Once you know how to read the names of the ETFs you will be able to search them more easily.

The keywords may be present in different order or some elements may be missing, but the principle remains.

Let's take a look at some real examples of ETF names to explain the meaning of the keywords.

Issuer

Who issues the ETF? The brand name of the ETF issuer is usually found at the beginning. For example, iShares Core EURO STOXX 50 UCITS ETF. Issuers of ETFs are commonly subsidiaries of large banks or wealth managers. iShares is part of BlackRock, the world's largest wealth manager, while Xtrackers is the brand of Deutsche Bank's ETF and Lyxor belongs to Société Générale.

Base range

The issuer name can also be deciphered by a sub-brand such as Core in the example above. This shows that the ETF is part of a sub-group of a range of the issuer's products. Terms such as Core are worth noting as these products are usually very cheap and generally based on key portfolios such as the EURO STOXX 50 index and MSCI World.

Core and Prime are sometimes used as terms in index names, such as "MSCI USA Prime Vale". In this case, the name has nothing to do with a reference to any particular inexpensive product.

Index

Where do you invest? The second component is the index replicated by the ETF. For example: iShares Core EURO STOXX 50 UCITS ETF.

Well-known index providers include MSCI, FTSE, STOXX and S&P. These provide independent verification of the indexes and licenses them to ETF providers. Often the name of the index reflects the region and the number of stocks followed. For example, the EURO STOXX 50 replicates the 50 largest companies traded in the eurozone.

You may also notice indexes with a suffix such as NR, TR or TRN. NR stands for Net Return, TR stands for Total Return and TRN stands for Total Return Net.

The suffixes tell us whether the index performance is calculated before or after dividend taxes. However, this has no direct impact on the performance of the ETF itself which distributes the dividends due to you.

Regulatory Information Important for Consumer Protection

Always look for the words UCITS in the name of your ETF, as in: iShares Core EURO STOXX 50 UCITS ETF. This abbreviation tells us that the ETF is subject to European regulations specifically designed to protect private investors.

UCITS ETFs must meet certain standards such as not holding more than 20% of the fund's assets in a single financial instrument, in order to facilitate product diversification. The term ETF also represents a regulatory classification. It clearly differentiates ETFs from other exchange-traded products such as ETCs (Exchange Traded Commodities) or ETNs (Exchange Traded Notes).

ETCs and ETNs do not comply with UCITS rules and are subject to additional risks which do not affect ETFs. Before investing in these products make sure you have done thorough research.

Share class

Near the end of the ETF name you will usually find a cryptic abbreviation that provides information on the asset class such as: Xtrackers S&P 500 UCITS ETF 1C.

ETFs often issue different classes of shares. Share classes are variants of the fund that may differ based on fees, trading, currency or return distribution method. You can accurately identify the variant you want from its unique 12-digit ISIN code. Unfortunately, however, each broadcaster uses its own list of abbreviations for this reason it is not possible to decipher it quickly.

The yield paid in the form of dividends or interest can be sent either directly through the brokerage account or automatically reinvested in the ETF in order to increase your share more quickly.

Return paying ETFs are known to be "distributing", such as: iShares FTSE MIB UCITS ETF (Dist). ETFs that reinvest yield are termed "accumulation", such as: iShares FTSE MIB UCITS ETF (Acc).

Distributing ETFs have one of the following abbreviations:

- D
- Dis
- Dist

Accumulation ETFs usually contain one of the following abbreviations:

- C
- Acc

Currency ETFs that invest in eurozone equities carry a currency risk. If the name of the ETF indicates that it is hedged in EUR, this product will be protected against currency fluctuations through the use of forward contracts or options. In the case of Lyxor S&P 500 UCITS ETF Daily Hedged D-EUR, a Euro investor will earn the return of the US index as the hedging will eliminate the effect of the euro's performance against the dollar.

If the currency is known but the term "hedged" is not present, this usually indicates that the ETF is traded in that currency.

Some ETF providers prefer to emphasize the fact that their ETFs are domiciled in Ireland. Why? Because an Irish domicile can offer a tax advantage to some investors. The abbreviation "IE" in UBS ETF names is a great example of this. Be careful when you notice: Short, 2x Leveraged. These risky ETFs allow investors to multiply index movements by a factor of two or three.

ETFs that benefit from falling prices are often referred to as short ETFs.

Be very careful with leveraged products. These are very risky and are specific investments that should only be used by very experienced investors who fully understand how they work.

ETF names are often ambiguous at first glance but you will soon be able to decode them once you master this information.

Conclusion

Congratulations on making it to the end of this book, we hope you found some useful insights to take your stock investing skills to the next level. As you should know by now, the world of stocks is extremely complicated and there is a new "opportunity" every way you look. However, our experience tells us that only by taking things seriously and having a proper plan you can develop your investing skills to the point that you can actually accumulate wealth.

Our final advice is to stay away from the shining objects that the world of stocks offers you every day. Simply dollar cost average into a broad ETF and study the world of stocks in depth. After you have sufficient knowledge on what you are talking about, you can go ahead and invest into single companies. Analyze your results, improve your money management skills and become the master of your emotions.

As you can see, there are no shortcuts you can take. Easy money does not exist. What exists is the possibility to start from zero and work your way up to become a professional stock investor. The journey might be difficult, but it is certainly worth it.